Life at McPherson High

Campus Life Books

After You Graduate
Against All Odds: True Stories of People Who Never Gave Up
Alive: Daily Devotions
Alive 2: Daily Devotions
The Campus Life Guide to Dating
The Campus Life Guide to Making and Keeping Friends
The Campus Life Guide to Surviving High School
Do You Sometimes Feel Like a Nobody?
Life at McPherson High
The Life of the Party: A True Story of Teenage Alcoholism
The Lighter Side of Campus Life
A Love Story: Questions and Answers on Sex
Making Life Make Sense
Peer Pressure: Making It Work for You
Personal Best: A Campus Life Guide to Knowing and Liking Yourself
Welcome to High School
What Teenagers Are Saying about Drugs and Alcohol
Worth the Wait: Love, Sex, and Keeping the Dream Alive
You Call This a Family? Making Yours Better

Life at McPherson High

JOHN McPHERSON

A DIVISION OF CTi
CampusLife
BOOKS

ZondervanPublishingHouse
Grand Rapids, Michigan
A Division of HarperCollinsPublishers

Life at McPherson High
Copyright © 1991 by John McPherson
All rights reserved

Campus Life books are published by
Zondervan Publishing House
Grand Rapids, Michigan 49530

Library of Congress Cataloging-in-Publication Data

McPherson, John, 1959–
    Life at McPherson High / John McPherson.
      p. cm.
    ISBN 0-310-71161-4 (paper)
      1. High school students—Caricatures and cartoons.
      2. American wit and humor, Pictorial. I. Title.
NC1429.M275A4 1991
741.5'973—dc20   90–20298
                                            CIP

Printed in the United States of America

92 93 94 95 96 / CH / 10 9 8 7 6 5 4 3 2

For Mom and Dad

Special thanks to Chris Lutes,
without whose encouragement,
editorial wisdom, and laughter
this book would never have made
it off the drawing board.

CLASSES

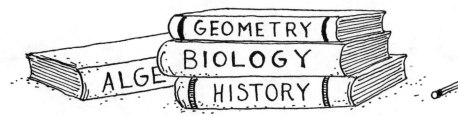

AS SOON AS HIS DAD BOUGHT THE VIDEO CAMERA, ERIC KNEW THAT THE FIRST DAY OF SCHOOL WOULD BE A CATASTROPHE.

MRS. MUTNER WENT OVER A FEW OF HER RULES ON THE FIRST DAY OF SCHOOL.

JIM SCHAAD WAS ONE OF THE FEW PEOPLE IN THE SCHOOL WHO COULD BURP THE ENTIRE STAR TREK THEME SONG.

"EXCUSE ME, MRS. NELTIK. WE HAD A BIOLOGY PROJECT GET A LITTLE OUT OF CONTROL NEXT DOOR. DID YOU BY ANY CHANCE SEE A GREEN AND RED SNAKE, ABOUT 6 OR 7 FEET LONG...OH, THERE HE IS!"

THIS WAS THE THIRD TIME IN A WEEK
THAT GREG GOT CAUGHT PASSING NOTES TO LIZ.

LYLE'S ABILITY TO TIE FLIES TO
LINDA SANDUSKY'S HAIR EARNED HIM
37 WEEKS OF DETENTION STUDY HALL.

BIOLOGY LAB

"SO, HOW WAS CHEM LAB?"

"EXCUSE ME, MR. NURMOND? CAN I TALK TO YOU ABOUT A LITTLE PROBLEM I RAN INTO ON MY BIOLOGY PROJECT?"

"BEFORE WE BEGIN TODAY'S DISSECTION LAB, I'D LIKE YOU EACH TO SELECT YOUR SPECIMEN AND TAKE IT BACK TO YOUR LAB TABLE."

"YOU'RE RIGHT! IT DOES LOOK
LIKE PETE CLARK!"

MICROBIOLOGY
MR. LURWAD

McPHERSON

"THIS ISN'T WHAT I HAD IN MIND WHEN I SIGNED UP FOR SHOP CLASS."

KELLY BOWMAN'S TECHNIQUE FOR LATE PAPER EXCUSES WAS TO BABBLE INCESSANTLY UNTIL THE TEACHER GAVE IN.

WALT MESSES UP HIS RIGHT TURN SIGNAL ONCE AGAIN.

RECENT BUDGET CUTS HAD MADE A DRASTIC EFFECT ON THE MEEKER HIGH DRIVER ED. PROGRAM.

STUDY TIP: SAVE TIME ON BIG READING ASSIGNMENTS BY READING EVERY OTHER WORD.

THE MAGNA
CARTA WAS SIGNED IN
1215.

WAYNE MERLMAN COULDN'T FIND A HI-LIGHTER, SO HE USED
A BLACK MAGIC MARKER TO CROSS OUT ALL THE STUFF HE DIDN'T
WANT TO READ AGAIN.

TEACHERS

LORETTA WAS STARTING TO THINK THAT
BEING THE TEACHER'S PET WASN'T ALL
IT WAS CRACKED UP TO BE.

IT DIDN'T TAKE MUCH TO UPSET MRS. BURNSNARD.

MRS. MORTLEMAN MADE SURE THAT EVERYONE PARTICIPATED IN CLASS.

CHRIS JUDD WILL KNOW BETTER THAN TO RAISE HIS HAND THE NEXT TIME MR. NORWOOD ASKED FOR A VOLUNTEER TO ERASE THE BLACKBOARD.

MR. GLEMPLY WAS A MASTER OF REVERSE PSYCHOLOGY.

MR. GICKMAN WASN'T TOO GOOD WITH NAMES.

IT WASN'T LONG BEFORE STUDENTS STARTED TO TAKE ADVANTAGE OF MRS. GRINDLE'S NEARSIGHTEDNESS.

"SO, ANYWAY, RHONDA TOLD DORIS ALL ABOUT WAYNE AND...."

OUT IN THE HALLS

SEVERAL STUDENTS HAD THREATENED TO QUIT UNLESS
THE PRINCIPAL DROPPED HIS NEW DRESS CODE POLICY.

GOING TO THE SAME SCHOOL AS YOUR YOUNGER
BROTHER CAN BE AN AGONIZING EXPERIENCE.

"I'M TRYING TO AVOID BEING ASSOCIATED WITH ANY ONE PARTICULAR PEER GROUP."

HIGH-TOP SNEAKERS WERE BECOMING THE ULTIMATE STATUS SYMBOL AT MUELLER HIGH.

"PERSONALLY, I'LL BE SORT OF GLAD WHEN THIS FAD DIES OUT."

SPROING!

BOING!

McPHERSON

ONE OF THE HOTTEST FADS EVER TO HIT
BIMSLEY HIGH: TRAMPOLINE SHOES.

MIKE OHLER WAS SICK AND TIRED OF FORGETTING HIS LOCKER COMBINATION.

EXAMS

"LEON! KEEP YOUR EYES ON YOUR OWN PAPER!!"

EVERY HIGH SCHOOL STUDENT'S WORST ENEMY:
THE ESSAY QUESTION.

MRS. BRADT HOPED THAT ORAL MIDTERMS IN SPANISH 201 WOULD GIVE STUDENTS A UNIQUE CULTURAL EXPERIENCE.

AN S.A.T. SAMPLE QUESTION IS USED TO TEST STUDENTS' SENSE OF LOGIC.

SIX EXAMS IN 2½ DAYS HAD TAKEN THEIR TOLL ON PHIL WOGNARZ.

STUDY TIP: IF YOU'RE TAKING A COMPUTER SCORED TEST, BUT FORGOT TO BRING A NO.2 PENCIL, USE TWO NO.1 PENCILS INSTEAD.

S.A.T. PROCTORS ARE SPECIALLY TRAINED TO TERRORIZE STUDENTS BY CONTINUOUSLY WRITING DOWN THE TIME LEFT IN THE EXAM.

S.A.T. PRESSURE FINALLY PUSHES
TED SHUSTER OVER THE EDGE.

OUT TO LUNCH

STUDENTS' REQUESTS FOR MORE VARIETY
IN THE SCHOOL MENU CONTINUED TO GO UNHEEDED.

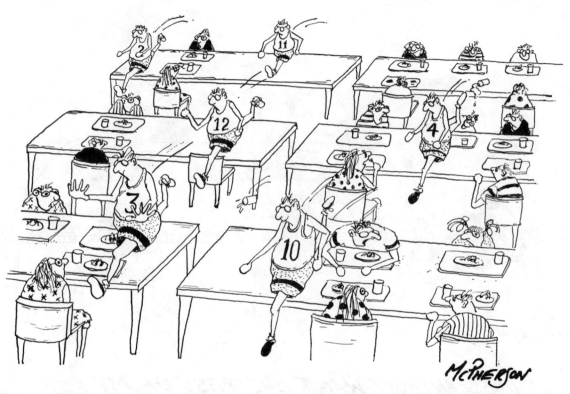

"I HATE IT WHEN THE TRACK TEAM COMES TO LUNCH."

"DOES ANYBODY WANT THE REST OF MY PEANUT BUTTER, MUSTARD, AND ASPARAGUS SANDWICH?"

"GARCÓN!"

NEEDLESS TO SAY, 98% OF THE STUDENTS AT MILPOT HIGH BROUGHT THEIR OWN LUNCHES.

IT WAS ABOUT TIME SOMEBODY PUT UP SOME
NO-PEST STRIPS IN THE THATCHER HIGH CAFETERIA.

RUMOR HAD IT THAT THERE WAS GOING TO BE A MASSIVE FOOD FIGHT DURING 6TH PERIOD LUNCH.

DAVE'S LATEST METAL SHOP PROJECT
REVOLUTIONIZED FOOD FIGHTS.

EXTRACURRICULAR ACTIVITIES

GET INVOLVED!
JOIN A CLUB!
- YAHTZEE CLUB
- FUTURE JANITORS OF AMERICA
- LIMBO DANCERS' CLUB
- TAG TEAM TETHERBALL
- FUN WITH LOGARITHMS
- STUDENTS FOR BETTER EYEGLASS CARE.
- CALCULATOR REPAIR AND MAINTENANCE
- STUDENTS AGAINST BAD BREATH

McPHERSON

DESPERATE TO SELL MORE PAPERS, THE NEWSPAPER STAFF AT LUTNER HIGH STOOPS TO THE LOWEST FORM OF JOURNALISM.

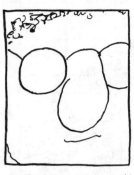

LEO HAMBO BARB HERD MORT DAVE HITCHCOCK SUEHOOP ER LIZ

McPHERSON

NOBODY WAS TOO PLEASED WITH THE
YEARBOOK STAFF AT WHATNEY HIGH.

"VERY GOOD, KATHY. THAT IS THE CORRECT SPELLING OF 'CARROT.' DON, WOULD YOU PLEASE SPELL 'PSEUDOPARENCHYMA.'"

UNABLE TO RAISE ENOUGH MONEY FOR A TEN-DAY
TRIP TO PARIS, THE MUCKLER HIGH FRENCH CLUB
HAD TO SETTLE FOR THREE DAYS IN CLEVELAND.

THE NUMBER-ONE ALL-TIME STUPIDEST SONG TO REQUEST AT A HIGH-SCHOOL DANCE.

THE LATEST IN STEREO TECHNOLOGY:
THE PARTY WALKMAN.

AN EARLY VERSION OF THE WALKMAN.

SPACE ★ MANIACS

PSYCHO BUZZARDS

FZZZT!

McPHERSON

P. E.

DEEP DOWN INSIDE, COACH KNOTT HAD ALWAYS WANTED TO BE A MATH TEACHER.

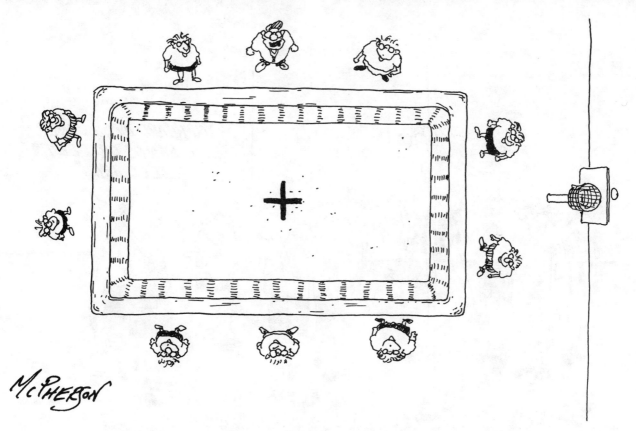

"LET GO OF THE CEILING, WILKINS!"

McPHERSON

HOW TO TELL WHEN IT'S TIME TO CHANGE YOUR GYM SOCKS.

LLOYD USES A POWERFUL SELF-DEFENSE TECHNIQUE.

JOCKS

THE ATHLETIC PROGRAM AT MILFOIL HIGH
NEEDED SOME SERIOUS UPGRADING.

"COACH SAYS NEXT YEAR WE'LL HAVE ENOUGH MONEY TO GET REAL HELMETS."

"IF YOU WANT MY OPINION, I THINK OUR COLOR GUARD IS OUT TO LUNCH."

TWANG!

THUNK!

DUE TO RECENT BUDGET CUTS, ROBERSON HIGH WAS
FORCED TO COMBINE ITS CROSS COUNTRY AND ARCHERY PROGRAMS.

BEING A CHEERLEADER FOR THE CROSS-COUNTRY
TEAM WAS NOT AN EASY TASK.

NEXT YEAR THE TEAM HOPED TO BUY OFFICIAL BACKBOARDS.

MORALE ON THE WADLEY HIGH BASKETBALL TEAM STARTED TO SLIP DURING THE PRE-GAME MEETING.

THE SMELDNER HIGH CHEERLEADERS DID LITTLE TO BOOST THE TEAM'S MORALE.

WALT OWED THIS VICTORY TO 10 YEARS OF BOY SCOUT TRAINING.

CHEERLEADING
REHEARSAL
HERE AT
4:00PM TODAY

McPHERSON

AS MEMBERS OF THE BOWLING TEAM, THE ROBB BROTHERS KNEW THIS WAS A ONCE IN A LIFETIME OPPORTUNITY.

SOMEBODY SABOTAGED THE FERBERVILLE
HIGH 440-RELAY TEAM BY PUTTING
SUPER-GLUE ON THEIR BATON.

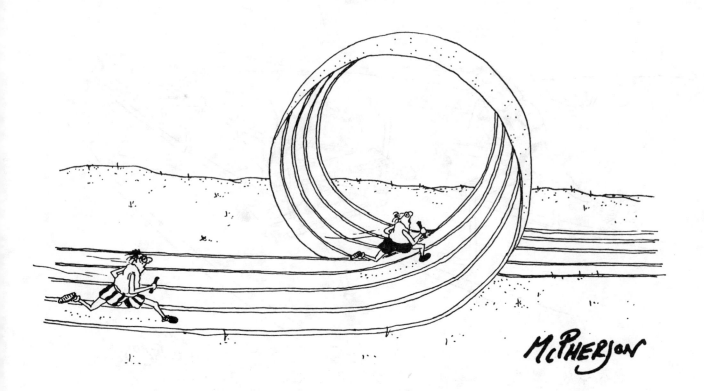

McPHERSON

THE HIGH HURDLES WERE NOT GLENN'S STRONGEST EVENT.

"THIS NEW TRAINING METHOD HAS INCREASED THEIR JUMPS BY 70%."

NO ONE COULD SLIDE LIKE JUSTIN "THE MOLE" FRAWLEY.

THE UMPIRES WERE STARTING TO SUSPECT THAT ZACK MIGHT BE THROWING A SPITBALL.

DATING

STELLA'S FATHER SHOULD HAVE KNOWN BETTER THAN TO ANSWER THE PHONE WHEN SHE WAS HOPING FOR A CALL FROM POTENTIAL PROM DATES.

NEEDLESS TO SAY, CHUCK'S SERENADING DIDN'T GET HIM A DATE WITH JEANNIE.

JAMEE HAD MADE A SERIOUS SCHEDULING ERROR.

"PSST! MAKE SURE YOU GET HER HOME BY TWELVE."

McPHERSON

THE BLIND DATE THAT WAS DESTINED TO FAIL.

ANOTHER DATE RUINED BY AN
EMBARRASSING COMMERCIAL.

"SO, YOU'RE OFF TO THE
BIG PROM TONIGHT, EH?
WHOOPS! SORRY ABOUT THAT."

AS AN EXPRESSION OF HIS DEEP LOVE FOR HER,
DAVE MADE JAMEE A PROM DRESS IN WOODSHOP.

AS ALWAYS, THE ANNUAL HIP-BOOT FORMAL AT MATTONE HIGH WAS A BIG SUCCESS.

LOUISE WAS STARTING TO DROP SOME SUBTLE
HINTS THAT SHE DIDN'T WANT TO SEE VERN ANYMORE.

RATHER THAN LEAD WALT ON, LOIS THOUGHT IT BEST TO BE UP FRONT ABOUT HER DECISION TO BREAK UP WITH HIM.

THE HOLIDAYS

IT DIDN'T TAKE PEOPLE LONG TO DISCOVER THAT THE SMIDLEY HIGH CHRISTMAS COMMITTEE HAD MISTAKENLY DECKED THE HALLS WITH BOUGHS OF POISON IVY.

SAY! ISN'T THAT MISTLETOE?!

SO FAR NO ONE HAD FALLEN FOR HOWARD MUSLAP'S MISTLETOE TRICK.

STUDENTS IN MR. MUSKIN'S MATH CLASS SUDDENLY LOST THE SPIRIT OF CHRISTMAS WHEN THEY DISCOVERED THAT THE GIFTS HE HAD GIVEN THEM CONTAINED THEIR MIDTERM EXAMS.

LORETTA SLAGG, BURNFEST HIGH'S
VERSION OF THE GRINCH.

MRS. OXNARD'S END OF THE YEAR GIFT TO EVERYONE WHO PASSED HER CLASS MADE MOST OF THEM WISH THEY HADN'T.

EVERYONE IN MRS. SNURLMAN'S CLASS PITCHED
IN AND GOT HER THE ULTIMATE GIFT:
A GAS-POWERED BLACKBOARD ERASER.

PARENTS

BOB TRIED IN VAIN TO GET THROUGH THE LIVING ROOM WITHOUT SHOWING HIS REPORT CARD TO HIS PARENTS.

AS PUNISHMENT FOR HIS LOW GRADES, WAYNE'S MOTHER FORCED HIM TO WATCH 12 HOURS OF HEE HAW RERUNS.

LORRAINE'S WORST NIGHTMARE COMES TRUE.

WUMP!

M:PHERSON

A CURFEW WAS NOT SOMETHING TO BE TAKEN LIGHTLY IN THE MILLIGAN HOUSEHOLD.

"WALTER, WE WON'T HAVE TO BUY DOREEN A NEW PROM DRESS AFTER ALL. MY OLD PROM DRESS FITS HER PERFECTLY!"

BLAT!

McPHERSON

MR. MELNIK EXPRESSES HIS DISAPPROVAL OF WENDY'S NEW BOYFRIEND.

"LOOK, MOM AND DAD. ALL I WANT IS A LITTLE MORE INDEPENDENCE. IS THAT TOO MUCH TO ASK?"

WALLY NORTMAN WAS A MASTER AT BEATING CURFEWS.

SUMMER JOBS

BOB'S
RUBBER BAND
REPAIR SHOP

*CHOOSE FROM A WIDE VARIETY OF
NEW + USED RB'S!
* ASK ABOUT OUR GIFT CERTIFICATES!

*24 HOUR EMERGENCY REPAIR
SERVICE!

USED

M⸍PHERSON

*BOB'S NEW BUSINESS VENTURE WASN'T THE GOLD
MINE HE HAD THOUGHT IT WOULD BE.*

TED'S CHANCES OF GETTING A RAISE
WEREN'T LOOKING TOO HOT.

THURL'S WEED TRIMMING JOB AT MR. WIMPLE'S COMES TO AN ABRUPT HALT.

BUD FOUND A GREAT WAY TO EXPAND ON HIS SUMMER LAWN JOB.

GRADUATES

LOUIS WRZYNSKI'S LIFELONG FASCINATION WITH DOMINOES CULMINATED IN THIS ONE FATEFUL MOMENT.

CLASS OF 1991

McPHERSON

"I ALWAYS THOUGHT 'SHEEPSKIN' WAS JUST AN EXPRESSION."

"I DON'T HAVE TO RETURN THE CAP AND GOWN UNTIL WEDNESDAY, SO I FIGURED I MIGHT AS WELL GET SOME USE OUT OF THEM."

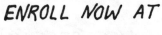

ENROLL NOW AT
ED'S UNIVERSITY!

ED MUTTLEY
PRESIDENT

- ONLY $700 PER SEMESTER!

- BUY 2 SEMESTERS, GET THE 3rd ONE AT HALF PRICE!

AND, IF YOU ORDER NOW, YOU'LL GET THE FOLLOWING COURSES ABSOLUTELY FREE!

1. COUNTING
2. INTERMEDIATE HAIRSTYLING
3. THE HISTORY OF BOWLING

STOP BY ED'S CAMPUS NOW AND RECEIVE A FREE ED'S U. TOTE BAG, NO PURCHASE NECESSARY!

*OFFER VOID WHERE PROHIBITED
*NOT AVAILABLE IN ANY STORES

SUMMER
VACATION

THE DREADED END-OF-THE-YEAR LOCKER CLEAN-OUT.

WITH SUMMER ON THE WAY, PEGGY WAS TRYING DESPERATELY TO GET A HEAD START ON HER TAN.

"THE SEAT THAT CAME WITH THE
BIKE WAS TOO DARNED UNCOMFORTABLE."

SUMMER WASN'T EVEN HALFWAY OVER, AND ALREADY THE DREADED SIGNS BEGAN TO APPEAR.

STUDENTS AT WAGNER HIGH WEREN'T READY TO ACCEPT THE FACT THAT SUMMER VACATION WAS OVER.